YOU CAN DRAW IT!

ALIENS

WRITTEN BY MAGGIE ROSIER
CONCEPTS AND ILLUSTRATIONS
BY STEVE PORTER

BELLWETHER MEDIA • MINNEAPOLIS, MN

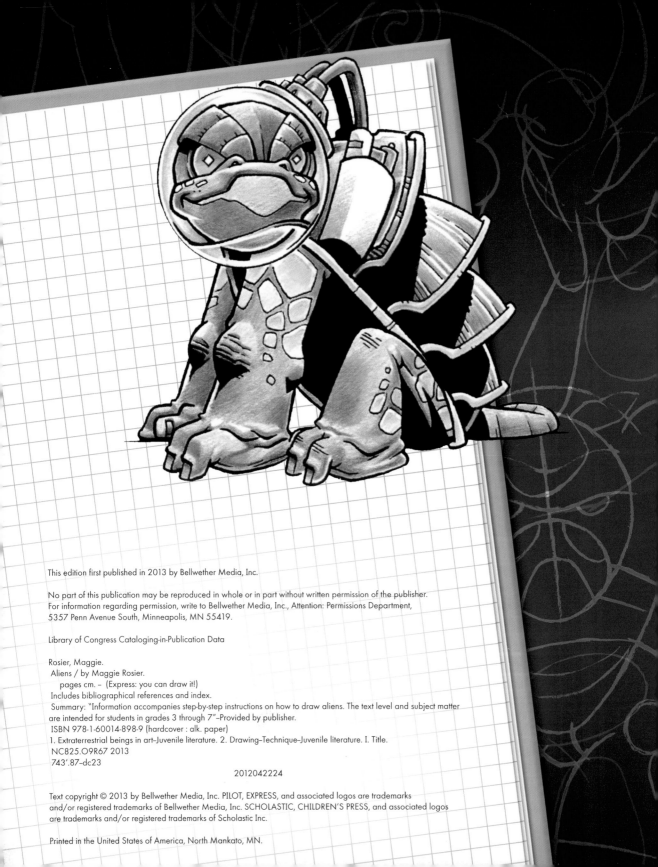

This edition first published in 2013 by Bellwether Media, Inc.

No part of this publication may be reproduced in whole or in part without written permission of the publisher.
For information regarding permission, write to Bellwether Media, Inc., Attention: Permissions Department,
5357 Penn Avenue South, Minneapolis, MN 55419.

Library of Congress Cataloging-in-Publication Data

Rosier, Maggie.
  Aliens / by Maggie Rosier.
    pages cm. – (Express: you can draw it!)
  Includes bibliographical references and index.
  Summary: "Information accompanies step-by-step instructions on how to draw aliens. The text level and subject matter
are intended for students in grades 3 through 7"–Provided by publisher.
  ISBN 978-1-60014-898-9 (hardcover : alk. paper)
  1. Extraterrestrial beings in art–Juvenile literature. 2. Drawing–Technique–Juvenile literature. I. Title.
  NC825.O9R67 2013
  743'.87–dc23
                           2012042224

Printed in the United States of America, North Mankato, MN.

TABLE OF CONTENTS

ALIENS!

The ground we stand on feels solid and sturdy, but planet Earth hangs in the universe as a defenseless speck. It is just one world in a vast field of solar systems, stars, and **galaxies**. We can only imagine what life forms exist beyond our reach!

DRAWING FROM OTHER ILLUSTRATIONS IS A GREAT PLACE TO START. WORK YOUR WAY UP TO DRAWING FROM YOUR IMAGINATION.

Before you begin drawing, you will need a few basic supplies.

PAPER

DRAWING PENCILS

2B OR NOT 2B?

NOT ALL DRAWING PENCILS ARE THE SAME. "B" PENCILS ARE SOFTER, MAKE DARKER MARKS, AND SMUDGE EASILY. "H" PENCILS ARE HARDER, MAKE LIGHTER MARKS, AND DON'T SMUDGE VERY MUCH AT ALL.

BLACK INK PEN

COLORED PENCILS
(ALL DRAWINGS IN THIS BOOK WERE FINISHED WITH COLORED PENCILS.)

ERASER

PENCIL SHARPENER

E.T.
The Earth Explorer

The highly intelligent E.T. is well known among humans because of its special interest in planet Earth. This **extraterrestrial** enters our atmosphere in a disc-shaped aircraft known by earthlings as a "flying saucer." Claims of alien **abduction** keep people guessing, but an E.T. shouldn't be feared. It is just as curious as we are!

1 START WITH SHAPES FOR THE HEAD AND BODY

2 ADD LINES FOR THE LEGS AND ARMS

LIGHT TO DARK

BEGIN YOUR DRAWING WITH VERY LIGHT LINES. SLOWLY BUILD UP TO DARK LINES AS YOU REACH THE FINAL STEPS OF YOUR DRAWING. THIS WILL ALLOW FOR EASY CORRECTION OF MISTAKES.

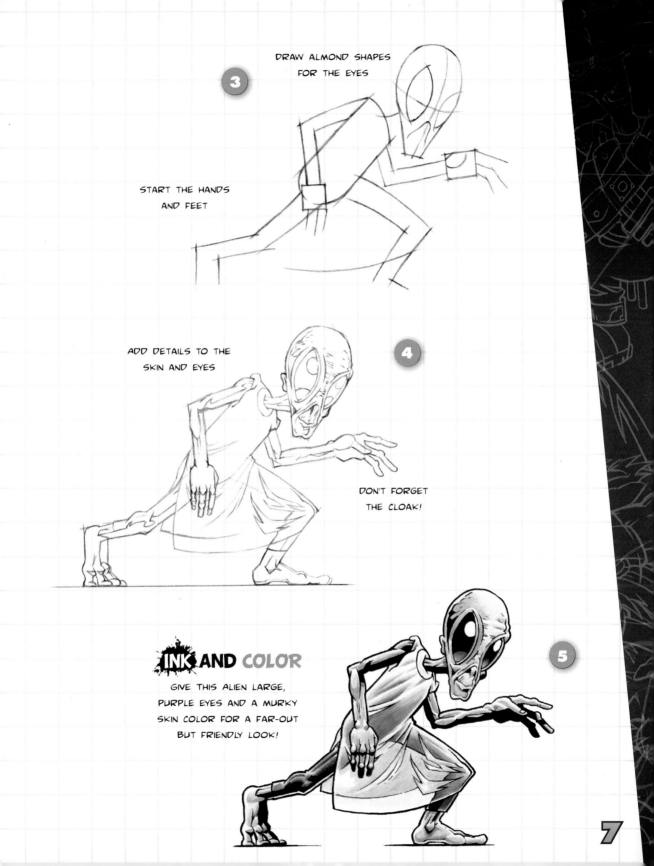

3

DRAW ALMOND SHAPES
FOR THE EYES

START THE HANDS
AND FEET

ADD DETAILS TO THE
SKIN AND EYES

4

DON'T FORGET
THE CLOAK!

INK AND COLOR

GIVE THIS ALIEN LARGE,
PURPLE EYES AND A MURKY
SKIN COLOR FOR A FAR-OUT
BUT FRIENDLY LOOK!

5

Grunkar
The Warring One

Grunkar is a **desolate** land of rocky **skylines** and constant war. The Grunkar tribes have little to do but fight. When they're not in combat, they are hand-cutting rocks into **lethal** weapons. Set foot on the dusty soil of Grunkar and you're as good as dust yourself.

JUST A HINT

IT'S NOT NECESSARY TO INCLUDE EVERY SCALE AND SPOT ON YOUR SUBJECT. A FEW SCATTERED DETAILS CAN GIVE THE EFFECT. YOU CAN FINISH YOUR DRAWING A LITTLE FASTER THIS WAY.

1

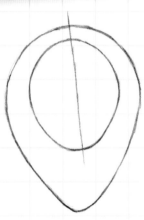

BEGIN THE DRAWING WITH AN EGG SHAPE AND A CIRCLE INSIDE

2

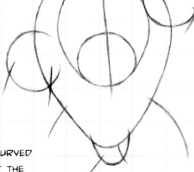

USE CIRCLES FOR THE SHOULDERS AND SNOUT

LIGHTLY SKETCH CURVED LINES TO START THE ARMS AND LEGS

3

START THE FACIAL FEATURES

DRAW THE REST OF THE ARMS AND LEGS

ADD BLOCK SHAPES FOR THE HANDS AND FEET

DON'T FORGET THE SWORD!

4

FINISH WITH FUR, TUSKS, AND CLAWS

5

INK AND COLOR

THIS GRUNKAR TRIBESMAN HAS FIERCE ORANGE EYES AND STEEL-GRAY SKIN. DON'T MESS WITH THIS ALIEN WARRIOR!

Mox
The Foreign Fixer

The planet of Morcoz hums with the busy bodies of its small inhabitants. They're called Mox, and they go nowhere without their full-body tool belts. These mini geniuses can fix anything, even if it belongs to strangers from a neighboring world. There's no better place to crash-land your spacecraft!

USE YOUR ARM

DRAW WITH YOUR WHOLE ARM, NOT JUST YOUR WRIST AND FINGERS.

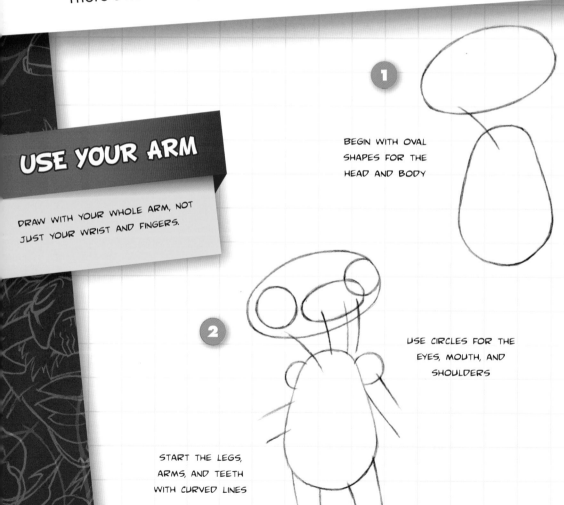

1 BEGIN WITH OVAL SHAPES FOR THE HEAD AND BODY

2 USE CIRCLES FOR THE EYES, MOUTH, AND SHOULDERS

START THE LEGS, ARMS, AND TEETH WITH CURVED LINES

3

USE BLOCK SHAPES
FOR THE HANDS

ADD THE FEET AND
TOOL BELTS

FINISH DETAILS ON THE
HANDS, FEET, AND FACE

4

DON'T FORGET ALL OF
THE HANDY TOOLS!

5

INK AND COLOR

THIS LITTLE GENIUS IS
PREPARED FOR ANYTHING
WITH THAT LOADED BROWN
TOOL BELT!

Bunks
The Intergalactic Hitchhiker

You are out cruising the **Milky Way** and something bangs into your spaceship. Maybe it's **space junk** or the beginnings of a **meteor shower**. If you're lucky, it is a Bunks. These roaming explorers are rare to come by. If you spot a drifting Bunks, pick it up. It's cosmic law!

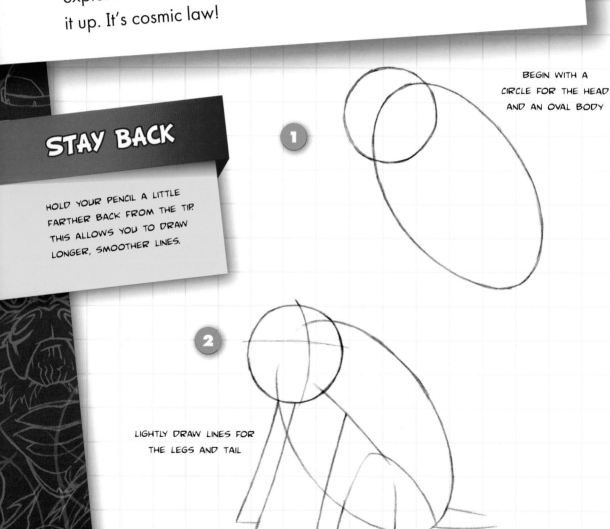

BEGIN WITH A CIRCLE FOR THE HEAD AND AN OVAL BODY

1

STAY BACK

HOLD YOUR PENCIL A LITTLE FARTHER BACK FROM THE TIP. THIS ALLOWS YOU TO DRAW LONGER, SMOOTHER LINES.

2

LIGHTLY DRAW LINES FOR THE LEGS AND TAIL

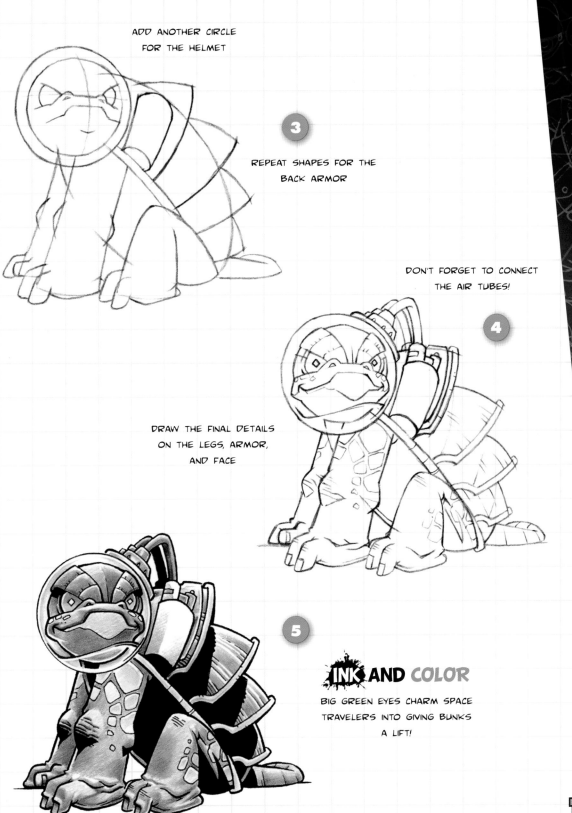

ADD ANOTHER CIRCLE
FOR THE HELMET

REPEAT SHAPES FOR THE
BACK ARMOR

3

DON'T FORGET TO CONNECT
THE AIR TUBES!

4

DRAW THE FINAL DETAILS
ON THE LEGS, ARMOR,
AND FACE

5

INK AND COLOR

BIG GREEN EYES CHARM SPACE
TRAVELERS INTO GIVING BUNKS
A LIFT!

Slee
The Deep-Sea Peacemaker

The troubled world of Turbadon has been **ravaged** by war for centuries. The Slee stays deep in the ocean and out of the fight. It is only when Turbadon is on the verge of total ruin that this wise **pacifist** intervenes. Its normally calm eyes flash in a bright fury that drives everyone to peace, if only for a while.

BREAK IT DOWN

JUST ABOUT ANY SUBJECT CAN BE BROKEN DOWN INTO SMALLER PARTS. LOOK FOR CIRCLES, OVALS, SQUARES, AND OTHER BASIC SHAPES THAT CAN HELP BUILD YOUR DRAWING.

1 START WITH A CIRCLE FOR THE HEAD AND A CURVY RECTANGLE FOR THE BODY

LIGHTLY DRAW THE BEGINNINGS OF THE CURVED ARMS AND NOSE

2 USE DIAGONAL LINES FOR THE TAIL END OF THE BODY

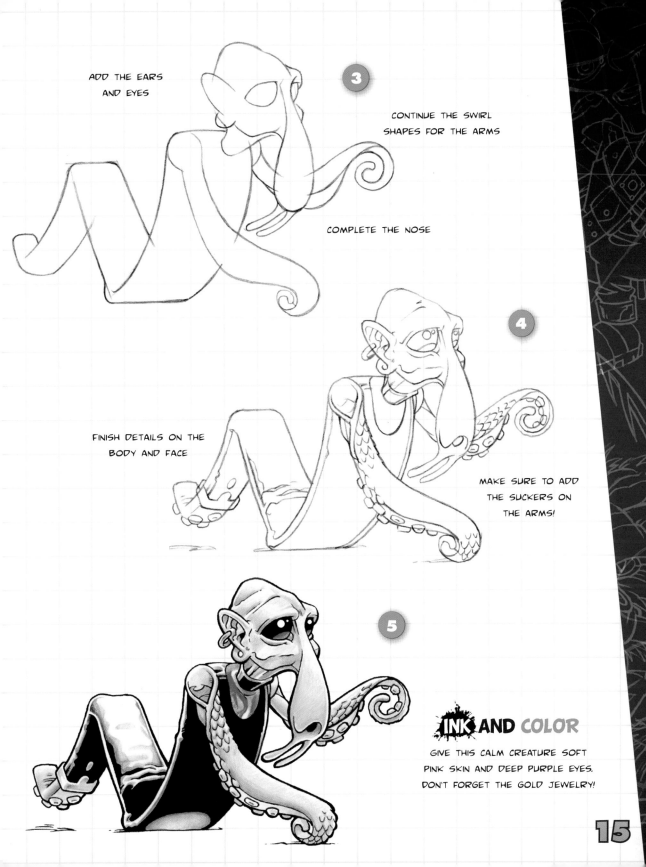

ADD THE EARS
AND EYES

3

CONTINUE THE SWIRL
SHAPES FOR THE ARMS

COMPLETE THE NOSE

4

FINISH DETAILS ON THE
BODY AND FACE

MAKE SURE TO ADD
THE SUCKERS ON
THE ARMS!

5

INK AND COLOR

GIVE THIS CALM CREATURE SOFT
PINK SKIN AND DEEP PURPLE EYES.
DON'T FORGET THE GOLD JEWELRY!

15

POK-N
The Pocket-Size Pest

One of the deadliest creatures you could encounter on an outer space adventure may also be the smallest. The destructive pea-sized POK-N isn't your average household pest. Try and stomp it out, and a broken foot will be the least of your worries. An angry POK-N won't hesitate to zap any threat to dust with its deadly laser cuffs.

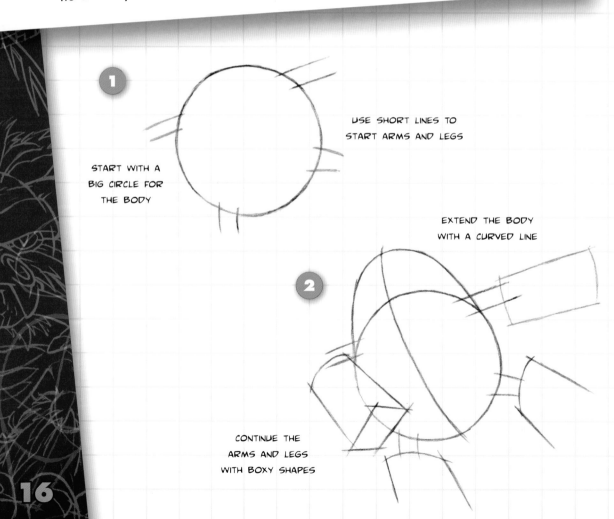

1

USE SHORT LINES TO START ARMS AND LEGS

START WITH A BIG CIRCLE FOR THE BODY

EXTEND THE BODY WITH A CURVED LINE

2

CONTINUE THE ARMS AND LEGS WITH BOXY SHAPES

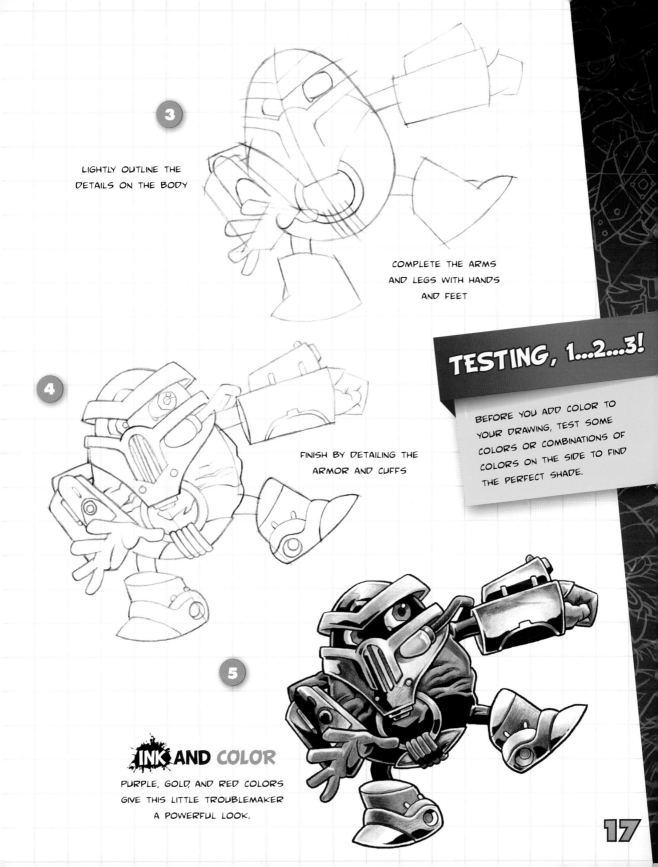

3

LIGHTLY OUTLINE THE
DETAILS ON THE BODY

COMPLETE THE ARMS
AND LEGS WITH HANDS
AND FEET

TESTING, 1...2...3!

BEFORE YOU ADD COLOR TO
YOUR DRAWING, TEST SOME
COLORS OR COMBINATIONS OF
COLORS ON THE SIDE TO FIND
THE PERFECT SHADE.

4

FINISH BY DETAILING THE
ARMOR AND CUFFS

5

INK AND COLOR

PURPLE, GOLD, AND RED COLORS
GIVE THIS LITTLE TROUBLEMAKER
A POWERFUL LOOK.

17

Wayleng
The Proud Protector

Earn the loyalty of a fifty-foot Wayleng and you're set for life. This alien species is a popular companion to the **elite** of many planets. It can sense **distress** from miles away and will come to your aid by land, sea, or sky. There's only one catch. Look a Wayleng directly in the eyes and its strong tail will wrap you up before you can blink!

SEE THE BIG PICTURE

WAIT TO ADD DETAILS UNTIL YOU ARE HAPPY WITH THE BASIC SHAPE OF YOUR DRAWING. YOU DON'T WANT TO SPEND TIME DETAILING A PART OF YOUR DRAWING THAT WILL BE ERASED LATER.

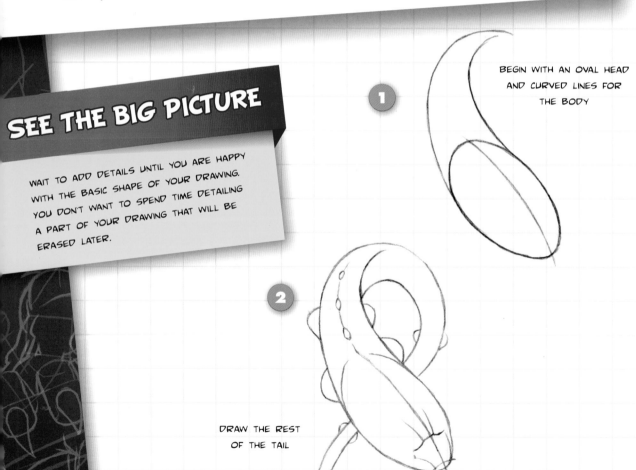

1 BEGIN WITH AN OVAL HEAD AND CURVED LINES FOR THE BODY

2 DRAW THE REST OF THE TAIL

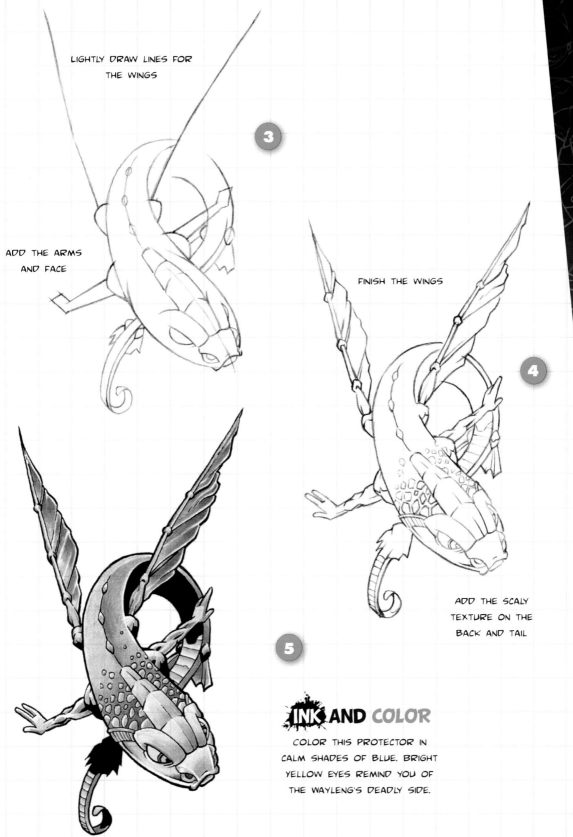

LIGHTLY DRAW LINES FOR THE WINGS

ADD THE ARMS AND FACE

3

FINISH THE WINGS

4

ADD THE SCALY TEXTURE ON THE BACK AND TAIL

5

INK AND COLOR

COLOR THIS PROTECTOR IN CALM SHADES OF BLUE. BRIGHT YELLOW EYES REMIND YOU OF THE WAYLENG'S DEADLY SIDE.

Ekeelo
The Silent Hunter

Millions of **light-years** away, the planet of Vertera bursts with tropical wildlife. Lurking silently beneath the dense jungle **canopies** is the Ekeelo. The lean body of this **hunter-gatherer** is built to slowly stalk prey. With a spear locked between its crushing fingers, the peaceful Ekeelo can turn deadly in an instant.

1

BEGIN BY DRAWING A CIRCLE FOR THE HEAD AND AN OVAL FOR THE BACK

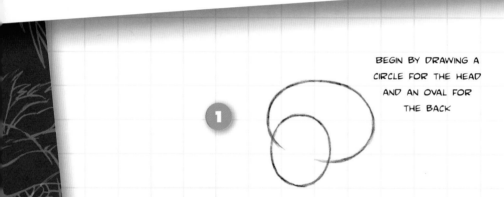

JUST WALK AWAY

IF YOU'RE STUCK ON A CERTAIN PART OF YOUR DRAWING, IT IS SOMETIMES BEST TO WALK AWAY. COME BACK LATER WITH A FRESH APPROACH!

2

ADD THE HIPS AND BODY

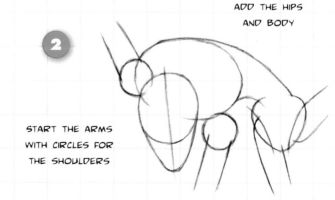

START THE ARMS WITH CIRCLES FOR THE SHOULDERS

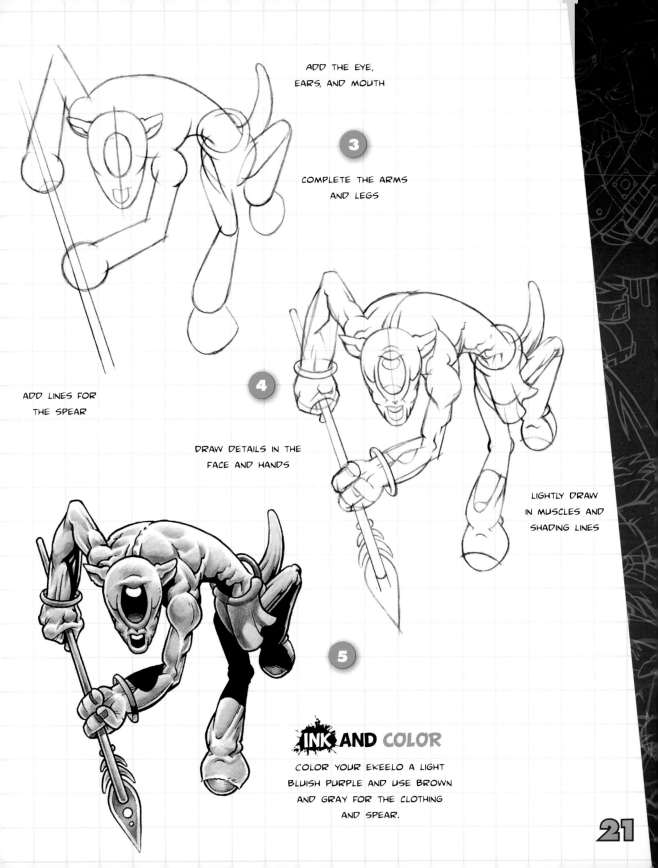

ADD THE EYE,
EARS, AND MOUTH

3

COMPLETE THE ARMS
AND LEGS

ADD LINES FOR
THE SPEAR

DRAW DETAILS IN THE
FACE AND HANDS

4

LIGHTLY DRAW
IN MUSCLES AND
SHADING LINES

5

INK AND COLOR

COLOR YOUR EKEELO A LIGHT
BLUISH PURPLE AND USE BROWN
AND GRAY FOR THE CLOTHING
AND SPEAR.

GLOSSARY

abduction—the act of taking someone by force

canopies—thick coverings of leafy branches formed by the tops of trees

desolate—empty and without joy or comfort

distress—pain or suffering

elite—those with great power, influence, or wealth

extraterrestrial—a being that comes from outside the Earth

galaxies—systems of stars, gas, and dust that are bound by gravity

hunter-gatherer—one who seeks wild animals and plants as a main source of food

lethal—deadly

light-years—units used to measure distance in space; a light-year is the distance that light travels in one year.

meteor shower—an event in which particles called meteoroids stream into Earth's atmosphere at high speeds; meteoroids are often no bigger than grains of sand.

Milky Way—the galaxy to which our solar system belongs; the Milky Way is made up of billions of stars.

pacifist—one who is against war

ravaged—damaged or destroyed

skylines—the lines that form where buildings or other structures seem to meet the sky

space junk—human-made objects that have been left in space and now orbit the Earth

At the Library

Erickson, Justin. *Alien Abductions*. Minneapolis, Minn.: Bellwether Media, Inc., 2011.

Halls, Kelly Milner. *Alien Investigation: Searching for the Truth About UFOs and Aliens*. Minneapolis, Minn.: Millbrook Press, 2012.

Reinagle, Damon J. *Draw Alien Fantasies*. Columbus, N.C.: Peel Productions, 1996.

On the Web

Learning more about aliens is as easy as 1, 2, 3.

1. Go to www.factsurfer.com.

2. Enter "aliens" into the search box.

3. Click the "Surf" button and you will see a list of related Web sites.

With factsurfer.com, finding more information is just a click away.

INDEX